Python Programming for Kids Between 6 to 13

Take The First Step Towards a Coding Future With Python Programming For Kids!

Tara T. Pierce

This work is copyrighted ©2023 by Tara T. Pierce All rights reserved. No part of this work may be reproduced or transmitted in any form or by any means, electronic or mechanical, including photocopying, recording, or by any information storage and retrieval system, without permission in writing from the copyright owner.

Python programming for kids between 6 to 13 is a unique learning program designed to help children understand the fundamentals of programming and help them develop basic coding skills. All content and materials associated with this program are the property of the copyright owner and should not be used without prior written permission.

Table of Contents

Chapter 1. What is Python?

Chapter 2. The Benefits of Python programming for Kids

Chapter 3. Why Python is a Great Language to Learn for Kids

Chapter 4. Getting Started with Python

Chapter 5. Learning the Basics of Programming

Chapter 6. Working with Files and Text

Chapter 7. Working with Graphics

Chapter 8. Working with the Web

Chapter 9. Encouragement to Keep Learning and Exploring

Introduction to Python

Are you looking to give your child a head start in the world of coding? Python programming for kids between the ages of 6 and 13 is a great way to introduce your child to the fundamentals of coding and programming.

With an intuitive and straightforward syntax, Python is an easy language to learn, allowing your child to pick it up quickly.

By learning Python programming, your child can take the first step towards a successful coding future!

Let's explore the basics of Python programming for kids and why it's a great choice for early-age coding.

Chapter 1. What is Python?

Python is a type of computer language that people use to tell computers what to do. Just like you use words and sentences to tell your parents or teachers what you want, programmers use Python to give instructions to computers.

For example, a Python program can be used to make a computer game or help organize and sort large amounts of data.

It can be used to automate repetitive tasks and it is a powerful tool for scientific research. It's like giving a robot a set of commands to follow, and it will do it for you, just like magic!

Chapter 2. The Benefits of Python programming for Kids

Python is a great programming language for kids to learn because it is easy to understand and use. Here are some of the benefits of learning Python:

Easy to learn: Python has a simple and straightforward syntax, which makes it easy for kids to understand and start coding right away. It is also a high-level programming language, which means that it is closer to natural language and doesn't require as much knowledge of computer systems as other languages.

Versatile: Python can be used for a wide range of tasks, from simple games and animations to more advanced projects such as data analysis and machine learning. This means that kids can continue to learn and use Python as they grow older and their interests and skills develop.

Active community: Python has a large and active community of users and developers. This means that there are many resources available for kids to learn from, such as tutorials and forums, and that they can also share their own projects and get feedback from others.

Good for problem-solving: Learning to code with Python helps children to develop problem-solving and critical thinking skills, as well as logic and creativity. The process of coding requires breaking down a problem into smaller pieces and figuring out how to solve each piece, which develops these skills.

Future career opportunities: Knowing how to code in Python can open doors to many different career opportunities in the tech industry. With the increasing demand for skilled programmers, it's a valuable skill for kids to have as they grow up.

Learning Python can be a fun and engaging way for kids to explore their curiosity and creativity while developing important skills that will benefit them in the future.

Chapter 3. Why Python is a Great Language to Learn for Kids

Python is a great language to learn for kids because it is easy to read and write. Imagine you are writing a story, but instead of using words, you are using code.

Python is like a special language that computers understand. Just like how you learn to read and write in school, learning Python will help you talk to computers and give them instructions.

One of the best things about Python is that it is used in many different fields, like science, engineering, and art.

This means that as you learn more Python, you can use it to create all sorts of cool things, like video games, animations, and even websites!

Another great thing about Python is that it is a "high-level" language, which means it is closer to human language and easier to understand than some other programming languages.

This means that you can focus on solving problems and creating cool things, instead of getting stuck trying to understand complicated code.

Python also has a large community of people who use it, which means there are lots of resources and helpful people online who can answer questions and give you ideas for projects.

Learning Python is a great way to start exploring the world of programming and technology. It's a fun and powerful tool that can help you create all sorts of interesting things, and it's a skill that will be useful in many different fields. Plus, it's a great way to use your imagination and creativity!

Chapter 4. Getting Started with Python

Python is a powerful and versatile programming language that is widely used in many different fields, such as science, engineering, and art.

How to Install Python on your computer

Installing Python on your computer is like adding a new tool to your toolbox. Just like how you use a hammer to pound nails and a screwdriver to turn screws, you will use Python to give instructions to your computer.

Here's a step-by-step guide on how to install Python on your computer:

Step 1: Go to the Python website. You can type "python.org" into your web browser and press enter.

Step 2: Look for the "Downloads" section on the website. This is where you will find the link to download the Python installer.

Step 3: Click on the link to download the installer. Make sure you download the version that is compatible with your computer's operating system.

Step 4: Once the download is complete, double-click on the installer file to start the installation process.

Step 5: Follow the instructions on the screen to complete the installation. This may include clicking "next" or "agree" buttons.

Step 6: Once the installation is complete, you will have Python on your computer.

From now on, you can use Python on your computer to write and run code. You can use a program called "IDLE" to write and run your Python code.

You can find it by searching for it on your computer or by looking in the folder where Python was installed.

And that's it! You now have Python on your computer and you can start using it to give instructions to your computer.

It's like having a magic wand that you can use to make your computer do all sorts of cool things!

How to use the interactive shell

An interactive shell is a program that lets you give commands to your computer and see the results. Think of it like a conversation with your computer, where you type in something and your computer responds.

To use an interactive shell, you first need to open it. On a Windows computer, you can do this by clicking on the Start menu and searching for "Command Prompt" or "PowerShell." On a Mac or Linux computer, you can usually find it by searching for "Terminal" in your Applications or Utilities folder.

Once the interactive shell is open, you'll see a blinking cursor. This is where you can start typing commands. For example, you can type "dir" (without the quotes) and press Enter to see a list of the files and folders in the current directory.

You can also navigate through your file system using the command "cd" (without the quotes) followed by the name of the folder you want to go to.

For example, if you want to go to the folder named "Documents" you can type "cd Documents" (without the quotes) and press Enter.

Another command you can use is "ls" (without the quotes), it will list the files and folders in the current directory on Mac and Linux computer.

You can also use the command "clear" (without the quotes) to clear the screen and start with a clean slate.

Try experimenting with different commands and see what happens. Remember that the interactive shell can be a powerful tool, but it's important to be careful and make sure you know what you're doing before you try anything new.

The Basic Syntax of Python

Python is a programming language that people use to make computer programs and tell computers what to do. It uses a certain way of writing called "syntax" that the computer can understand.

Here are some basic rules of the Python syntax that you should know:

Python uses indentation to show which lines of code belong together. This means that you should start a new line of code and press the space bar a few times to create a gap before you start typing.

Python uses a "#" symbol to indicate that a line is a comment. This means that the computer will ignore that line and it's only for the programmer to read and understand the code.

Python uses quotes (either single or double) to indicate that something is a string. A string is a type of data that is used to represent a word or a sentence. For example, "Hello, World!" is a string.

Python uses mathematical operators such as "+", "-", "*" and "/" to do mathematical calculations.

Python uses the "=" sign to assign a value to a variable. A variable is a name that stands for a value. For example, you can create a variable named "x" and give it the value 5 by writing "x = 5".

Python uses the keywords "if", "else", "elif" to make decisions in the code, this is called control flow.

Python uses the keyword "def" to define a function. A function is a block of code that performs a specific task when it is called.

Python uses the keyword "print" to display output on the screen.

Here's an example of a simple Python program that uses some of these basic elements:

```python
name = "Alice" # This line
assigns the string "Alice"
to the variable "name"
age = 7 # This line
assigns the number 7 to
the variable "age"

# This line uses the
"print" keyword to display
the value of the "name"
variable
print("My name is " +
name)

# This line uses the
"print" keyword to display
the value of the "age"
variable
print("I am " + str(age) +
" years old.")
```

This program assigns a value to two variables, then uses the "print" keyword to display the values of those variables on the screen.

There's a lot more to learn about Python syntax and programming in general, but these are the basics. Keep practicing and experimenting, and you'll be a Python pro in no time!

Chapter 5. Learning the Basics of Programming

Learning the basics of programming can be a great way to introduce children to the world of technology.

A. Variables and Data Types

A variable is like a box that you can put something in. Just like a real box can hold different things, like toys or snacks, a variable can hold different types of information, like numbers or words.

There are different types of information that a variable can hold, called data types. Some common data types are:

Numbers (like 3, 7, or 12)
Words (like "dog" or "banana")

True or false (like yes or no)

When you create a variable, you give it a name and decide what type of information it will hold.

For example, you could create a variable named "age" and give it the value of 7. Later, you could change the value of "age" to 8.

In programming languages, we declare a variable and assign values to it by using assignment operator '='. Example: age = 7, name = "John"

It's important to use good names for your variables so that you can remember what information they hold. It's also important to use the right data type for the information you want to store.

B. Control Flow Statements

Control flow statements are like special directions for a computer program. They tell the computer what to do next, depending on certain conditions.

For example, imagine you are playing a video game and you come to a fork in the road. One path leads to a treasure and the other leads to a monster. The control flow statement in the game would be like a sign that tells you which path to take.

In a computer program, there are different types of control flow statements like "if-else" and "for loop".

The "if-else" statement is like a question the computer asks. If the answer is "yes", the computer does one thing. If the answer is "no", it does something else.

A "for loop" is like a big circle that the computer goes around a certain number of times. Each time it goes around, it does a specific task.

Control flow statements help the computer make decisions and repeat tasks. It's kind of like how we make decisions and repeat tasks in our daily lives.

C. Loops

A loop is a special instruction in a computer program that tells the computer to repeat a certain task multiple times. Imagine you have a bucket of candies and you want to count them one by one. If you had to count them one by one, it would take a long time. But, using a loop, the computer can count them quickly and easily.

There are different types of loops in programming such as "for loop" and "while loop".

A "for loop" is used when you know how many times you want to repeat a task. It's like running around a track a certain number of times. The computer keeps track of how many times it has gone around and stops when it reaches the desired number.

A "while loop" is used when you want to repeat a task until a certain condition is met. It's like playing a game until you win. The computer will keep playing until it reaches the winning condition.

Loops are very useful in programming as they help in automating the repetitive task, and makes the programming more efficient.

D. Functions

A function is like a recipe in cooking. Just like how a recipe tells you how to make a certain dish, a function tells the computer how to do a certain task.

For example, let's say you want to make a cake. The recipe for the cake tells you what ingredients to use and in what order to mix them. The function is like the recipe but instead of ingredients, it uses instructions for the computer to follow.

Functions help you organize your code and make it easier to understand and use. You can use the same function many times in different parts of your program. This way you don't have to keep writing the same instructions over and over again.

Functions also help you test your code more easily. You can test each function separately, rather than trying to test everything at once.

Think of it as a code block, you can name it and use it multiple times instead of writing the same code again and again.

E. Modules

A module is like a big box filled with different tools. Just like how a tool box has different tools for different jobs, a module has different instructions for the computer to use.

For example, let's say you are building a birdhouse. You have a hammer, a saw, and nails in your tool box. These are the tools you need to build the birdhouse.

A module is like the tool box, it has different instructions or tools that you can use to make your program.

Modules make it easier for you to share your code with other people.

You can put all of your instructions in a module, and then other people can use those instructions in their own programs.

You don't have to create everything from scratch, you can use pre-existing modules and built-in libraries which can save a lot of time and effort.

Modules also help to organize your code, similar to how functions do. You can put related instructions together in one module. And you can also reuse the modules across different programs.

Think of it as a tool kit, you can use the tools inside it to make your program work, and you can also share it with your friends.

Chapter 6. Working with Files and Text

Working with files and text is an important part of programming. It allows you to read, write and manipulate data stored in files.

For example, you could write a program that reads a text file and counts the number of words in it. Or, you could write a program that creates a new text file and saves some information to it.

A. Opening and Reading Files

In Python, we can use the "open" function to open a file. The open function takes two arguments: the name of the file and the mode in which we want to open the file.

For example, we can open a file called "myfile.txt" in read mode like this:

```
file = open("myfile.txt", "r")
```

The "r" stands for read mode. There are other modes too, like "w" for write mode and "a" for append mode.

Once we have opened a file, we can read the contents of the file using the "read" function. For example:

```
content = file.read()
print(content)
```

This will print the contents of the file to the screen.

It's also important to close the file after we are done reading it. We can do this using the "close" function:

```
file.close()
```

You can also use the 'with' statement which handles the file closing automatically.

```
with open("myfile.txt",
"r") as file:
    content = file.read()
    print(content)
```

It's that simple! Now you can open, read, and close files in Python.

B. Writing and Saving Files

In Python, we can use the "open" function to create a new file or open an existing file. The open function takes two arguments: the name of the file and the mode in which we want to open the file.

For example, we can create a new file called "myfile.txt" in write mode like this:

```
file = open("myfile.txt", "w")
```

The "w" stands for write mode. It means that we can write something into the file.

Once we have opened a file in write mode, we can write the contents of the file using the "write" function. For example:

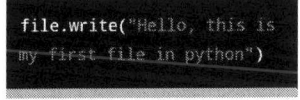

```
file.write("Hello, this is my first file in python")
```

This will write the sentence "Hello, this is my first file in python" in the file.

It's also important to close the file after we are done writing it. We can do this using the "close" function:

```
file.close()
```

You can also use the 'with' statement which handles the file closing automatically.

```
with open("myfile.txt",
"w") as file:
    file.write("Hello,
this is my first file in
python")
```

It's that easy! Now you can create, write and save files in Python easily.

C. Working with Text

Python is a great language for working with text! Here are a few ways you can use Python to work with text:

Printing text: You can use the print() function to print text to the screen. For example, you can print the message "Hello, World!" like this:

```
print("Hello, World!")
```

Storing text in variables: You can store text in variables, just like you can store numbers. For example, you can store the message "Hello, World!" in a variable called greeting like this:

```
greeting = "Hello, World!"
print(greeting)
```

Concatenating text: You can use the + operator to join two pieces of text together. For example, you can join the text "Hello, " and "World!" together like this:

```
part1 = "Hello, "
part2 = "World!"
greeting = part1 + part2
print(greeting)
```

Getting the length of text: You can use the len() function to find out how many characters are in a piece of text. For example, you can find out how many characters are in the text "Hello, World!" like this:

```python
greeting = "Hello, World!"
length = len(greeting)
print(length)
```

Indexing text: You can use square brackets [] to get a specific character from a piece of text. For example, you can get the first character of the text "Hello, World!" like this:

```python
greeting = "Hello, World!"
first_char = greeting[0]
print(first_char)
```

These are just a few examples of how you can work with text in Python. With a little bit of practice, you'll be able to do even more!

Chapter 7. Working with Graphics

Working with graphics in programming is like coloring and drawing with a computer! Instead of using a pencil or paintbrush, we use special code to create pictures on the computer screen.

For example, we can use Python to draw shapes like circles, rectangles, and triangles. We can also use it to add colors, patterns, and images to our drawings.

A. Introduction to PyGame

Pygame is a Python package that makes it simple to build games and interactive programs. Pygame allows you to build arcade games, puzzles, and even animations.

Pygame is a game development toolset. It features a variety of entertaining tools and functions that you may use to create your game. Pygame, for example, can be used to generate a moving character on the screen or a scrolling background.

You can pick and select what you need from the library to develop your game, just like you would with a real toolbox.

How to build a game with PyGame

Creating an arcade game with Pygame can be a fun and exciting project for kids! Here are the basic steps you can follow to create your own arcade game:

Setup: First, you'll need to install Pygame and set it up on your computer. You can do this by following the instructions on the Pygame website.

Planning: Before you start coding, it's a good idea to plan out your game. Think about what kind of game you want to create, and make a list of the different elements that you'll need, such as characters, backgrounds, and obstacles.

Design: Next, you can start designing your game. You can use a program like Paint to create the images and backgrounds for your game.

Coding: Now it's time to start coding your game. You can use Python and Pygame to create the different elements of your game, such as the character and the obstacles.

Testing: As you code, you should test your game to make sure it's working correctly. You can do this by running your game and playing through it.

Improving: Once you have a working game, you can continue to improve it by adding new features, fixing bugs, and making it more fun.

It's important to remember that creating a game can take a lot of time and effort.

Also, you can take a look at Pygame tutorials and sample codes, it will help you to understand how pygame works and how you can use it to create games.

B. **Drawing Shapes**

Drawing shapes in Python is a fun and easy way to create pictures on the computer screen!

There are many different shapes you can draw, such as circles, rectangles, and triangles.

To draw shapes in Python, you can use the library, Pygame. Pygame is a library that makes it easy to create games and fun interactive programs.

Here's an example of how you can use Pygame to draw a circle:

```python
import pygame

# Initialize Pygame
pygame.init()

# Set the size of the window
size = (700, 500)
screen = pygame.display.set_mode(size)

# Set the title of the window
pygame.display.set_caption("My Circle")

# Run the game loop
running = True
while running:
    for event in pygame.event.get():
        if event.type ==
```

```
pygame.event.get():
        if event.type ==
pygame.QUIT:
            running = False

    # Draw the circle
    pygame.draw.circle(screen, (255, 0, 0), (350, 250), 50)

    # Update the screen
    pygame.display.flip()

# Exit Pygame
pygame.quit()
```

This code creates a window with the title "My Circle" and draws a red circle with a radius of 50 pixels in the middle of the screen.

You can also use the draw.rect() function to draw rectangles, and the draw.polygon() function to draw triangles or any other shape.

Remember, you can use different colors and sizes to draw different shapes and create different patterns.

It's a fun way to explore programming and create your own drawings and designs. With a little bit of practice, you'll be able to create all kinds of cool shapes in Python!

C. Creating Animations

Creating animations in Python is a fun and exciting way to bring your pictures to life! Animations are like movies, but they are made with code instead of film.

To create animations in Python, you can use Pygame. Pygame is a library that makes it easy to create games and fun interactive programs.

Here's an example of how you can use Pygame to create a simple animation:

```python
import pygame

# Initialize Pygame
pygame.init()

# Set the size of the window
size = (700, 500)
screen = pygame.display.set_mode(size)

# Set the title of the window
pygame.display.set_caption("My Animation")

# Load the image
image = pygame.image.load("animation.png")

# Set the starting position of the image
```

```python
# Set the starting position of the
image
x = 0
y = 0

# Run the game loop
running = True
while running:
    for event in pygame.event.get():
        if event.type == pygame.QUIT:
            running = False

    # Clear the screen
    screen.fill((255, 255, 255))

    # Draw the image
    screen.blit(image, (x, y))
```

```python
    # Draw the image
    screen.blit(image, (x, y))

    # Move the image
    x += 1
    y += 1

    # Update the screen
    pygame.display.flip()

    # Wait for a bit
    pygame.time.wait(50)

# Exit Pygame
pygame.quit()
```

This code creates a window with the title "My Animation" and loads an image called "animation.png". It then moves the image across the screen and updates the screen to create the animation.

You can also use the time.sleep() function to control the speed of the animation.

Chapter 8. Working with the Web

Working with the web is all about using code to interact with the internet. It allows you to create websites, send and receive information, and interact with other websites.

There are many ways to work with the web using programming languages such as Python. Some examples include:

A. Working with the Requests Library

The requests library is a tool that allows you to easily send messages to websites and get information back. It's like sending a letter to a website and getting a letter back!

For example, imagine you want to get information from a website about a certain topic. You can use the requests library to send a message to the website asking for the information you want. The website will then send you back the information in a letter (or in computer terms, a response).

Here's an example of how you can use the requests library in Python to get information from a website:

```python
import requests

# Send a message to the website
response = requests.get("https://www.example.com")

# Print the letter (or response) we got back
print(response.text)
```

This code sends a message to the website "https://www.example.com" and gets back a response which is printed out.

You can also use the requests library to send information to a website, like filling out a form or sending a message. It's a very powerful tool for working with the web, and with a little bit of practice, you'll be able to use it to create fun and useful programs!

B. Working with APIs

APIs, or Application Programming Interfaces, are like secret codes that websites use to talk to each other. They allow different websites to share information and work together.

Imagine you want to get information from a website, but it's like a big castle with a lot of rooms and you don't know which room has the information you need. APIs are like a map or a key to the castle, they help you find the right room and get the information you need.

For example, a website that gives weather forecasts can have an API that allows other websites to access its weather data.

Here's an example of how you can use an API in Python to get information from a website:

```python
import requests

# Send a message to the website using the API
response = requests.get("https://api.example.com/weather?city=New+York")

# Print the response we got back
print(response.text)
```

This code sends a message to the website "https://api.example.com" using the weather API and gets back a response which is printed out.

APIs are a powerful way to get information from websites and use it in your own programs!

C. Creating Web Applications

Creating web applications is like building a house on the internet! Just like how you would build a house with rooms and furniture, you can use code to build a website with pages and buttons.

Web applications are programs that run on the internet and can be accessed by anyone with an internet connection. They can be used for all kinds of things, like shopping, playing games, or even learning new things.

To create a web application, you can use a programming language like Python and a web framework like Django or Flask. These frameworks provide the tools you need to create a website and handle things like user input and database storage.

Here's an example of how you can use Python and Flask to create a simple web application:

```python
from flask import Flask

app = Flask(__name__)

@app.route("/")
def hello():
    return "Hello, World!"

if __name__ == '__main__':
    app.run()
```

This code creates a web application that displays the message "Hello, World!" when you visit the home page.

Chapter 9. Encouragement to Keep Learning and Exploring

Learning and exploring is a never-ending journey, but it's a journey worth taking! Every time you learn something new, you open a door to new possibilities and new opportunities.

Python programming is a great tool to learn and explore, and with a little bit of practice and patience, you'll be able to create your own programs and see your ideas come to life.

Don't be discouraged if you come across difficulties along the way, they are normal and a part of the learning process. With each challenge you overcome, you'll become more confident and capable.

Remember, the most important thing is to keep going and to never give up. With each step you take, you'll become more proficient and knowledgeable in

Python programming, and you'll be able to create even more exciting and interesting programs.

So keep learning, keep exploring, and most importantly, have fun! With every new thing you learn, you'll be one step closer to achieving your goals and creating something truly amazing.

Conclusion

In conclusion, Python programming is an exciting and fun way for kids to learn how to code. It's a versatile language that can be used for all sorts of projects, from drawing shapes and creating animations to building web applications and working with the web.

Just like when you learn to play an instrument, practice is key to mastering Python. The more you play around with it, the better you'll become.

Python programming is like having a magic wand, you can use it to create anything you can imagine. You can create your own games, animations and even websites and share them with friends and family. It's a great way to express yourself creatively and have fun while learning a valuable skill.

Think of the possibilities, you could create an app that helps people find lost pets, a website that teaches kids how to code, or even a game.

Think of it like being a wizard, you have a spell book (the code) and you can cast spells (programs) to make things happen. It's a magical world of endless possibilities, and with Python, kids can be the master of their own digital realm.

So don't be afraid to dive into the world of Python programming, it's a fun and exciting journey filled with endless possibilities. Who knows, you might be the next tech wizard who creates the next big thing!